Looking at Maps and Globes

By Carmen Bredeson

Consultant
Nanci R. Vargus, Ed.D.
Primary Multiage Teacher
Decatur Township Schools, Indianapolis, Indiana

Children's Press®
A Division of Scholastic Inc.
New York Toronto London Auckland Sydney
Mexico City New Delhi Hong Kong
Danbury, Connecticut

Designer: Herman Adler Design
Photo Researcher: Caroline Anderson
The photo on the cover shows two children using a map and globe in a classroom.

Library of Congress Cataloging-in-Publication Data

Bredeson, Carmen.
Looking at maps and globes / by Carmen Bredeson.
p. cm. — (Rookie read-about geography)
Includes index.
Summary: This introductory book describes maps and globes, including the map legend, map scale, directions, equator, and North and South Poles.
ISBN 0-516-22351-8 (lib. bdg.) 0-516-25982-2 (pbk.)
1. Maps—Juvenile literature. 2. Globes—Juvenile literature. [1. Maps. 2. Globes.] I. Title. II. Series.
GA105.6 .B75 2001
912—dc21
00-060124

Printed in the United States of America.
1 2 3 4 5 6 7 8 9 10 R 10 09 08 07 06 05 04 03 02 01

Maps are flat drawings that show us where to find different places.

Long ago, the first maps were scratched into the dirt with a stick.

Today, most maps are printed on paper.

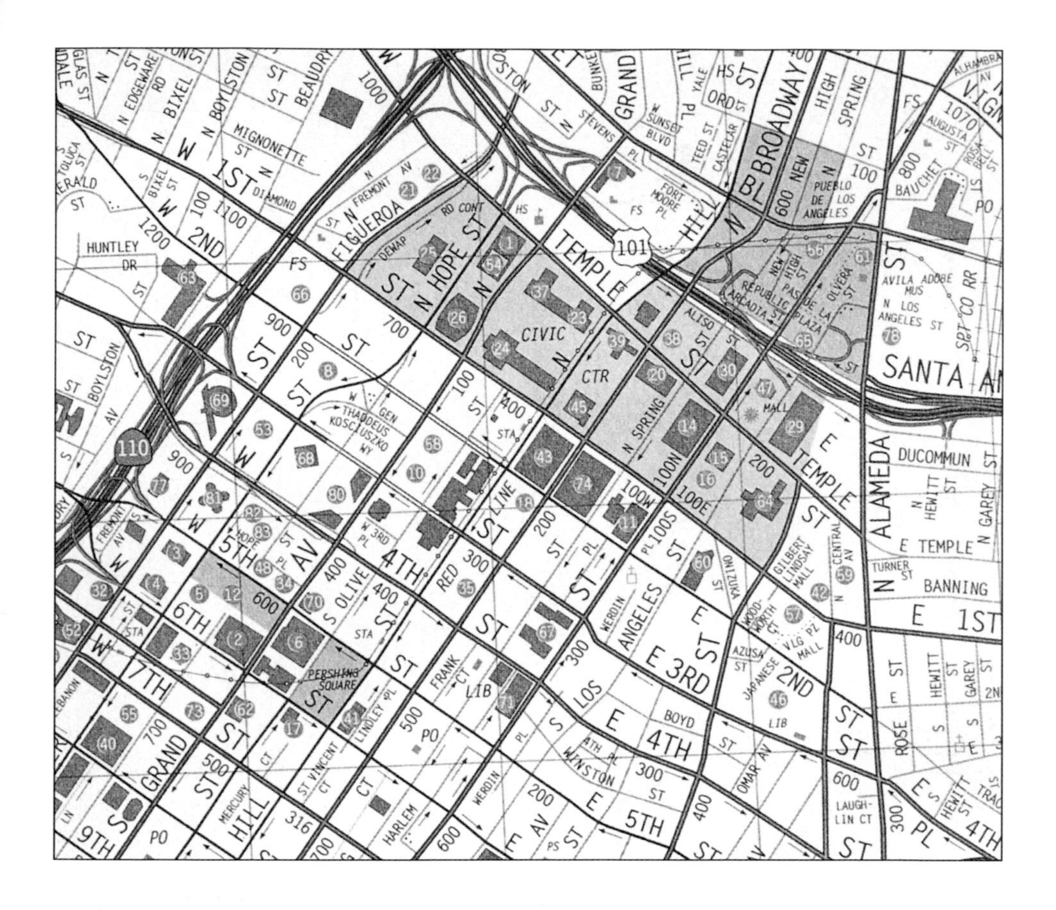

A map does not show exactly what something looks like.

It is not like a photograph.

Maps use symbols (SIM-buhls). Symbols are pictures that mean different things.

On this map, [mountain symbol] is the symbol for mountains. [tree symbol] is the symbol for a park.

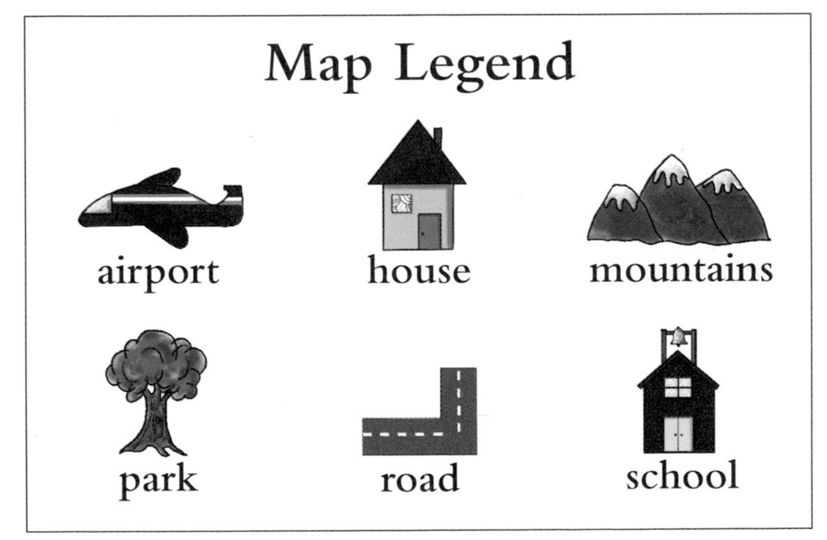
Map Legend
airport
house
mountains
park
road
school

The map legend (LEJ-end) shows what each symbol means.

Can you tell what the symbol for an airport is from this legend?

There are many kinds of maps. A world map shows the whole Earth. Some maps show just one town.

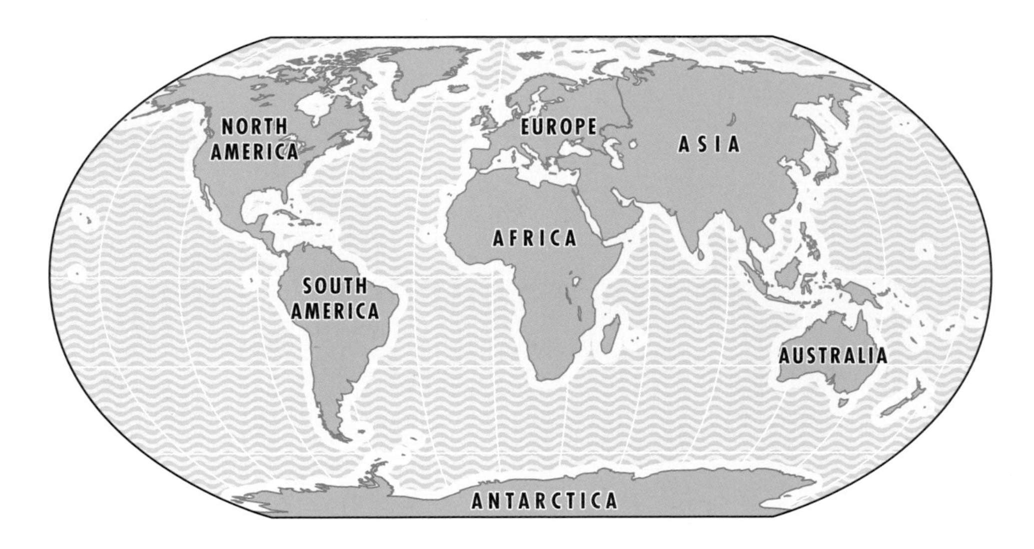

You can draw a map to show a new friend how to get to your house.

Road maps show us which road to take to get to another town.

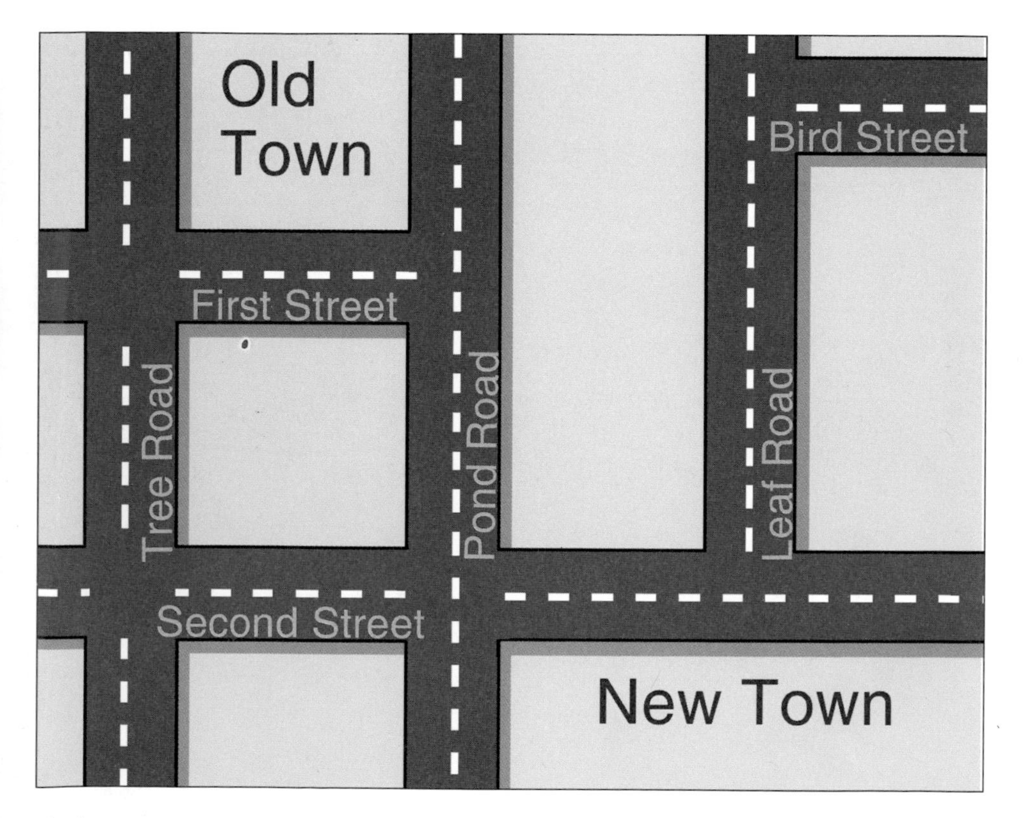

It is hard to fold a road map neatly!

We use the directions north, south, east, and west to read a map.

The top of a map is north. The bottom of a map is south. East is to the right. West is to the left.

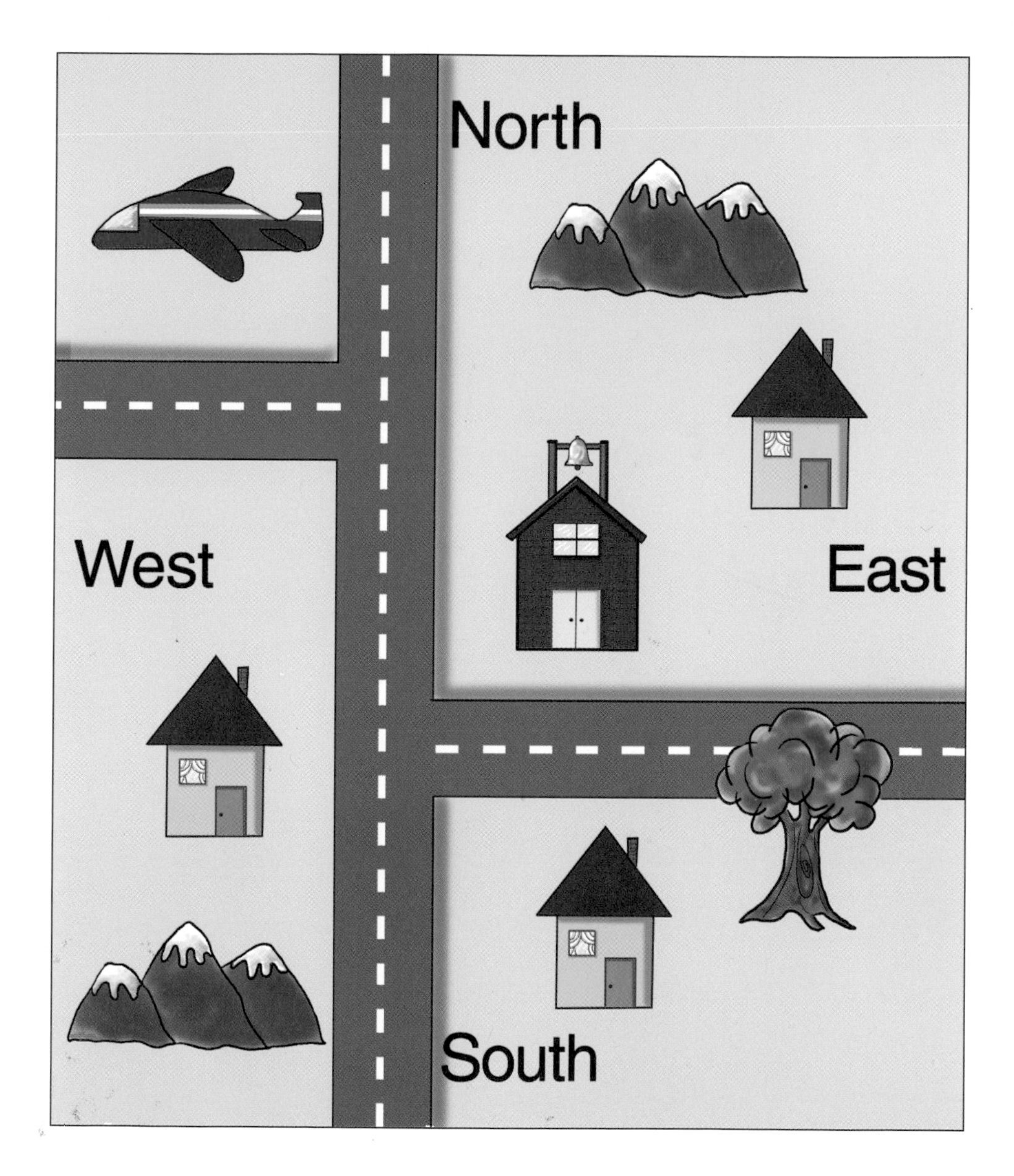
North
West
East
South

one inch

Maps cannot show the
real size of things.

One hundred miles on
Earth might take up just
one inch on a map.

The map scale shows us
how many real miles are
in one inch on the map.

On this scale, one inch
equals one mile.

That means that every
little inch on this map
is really one long mile
on Earth!

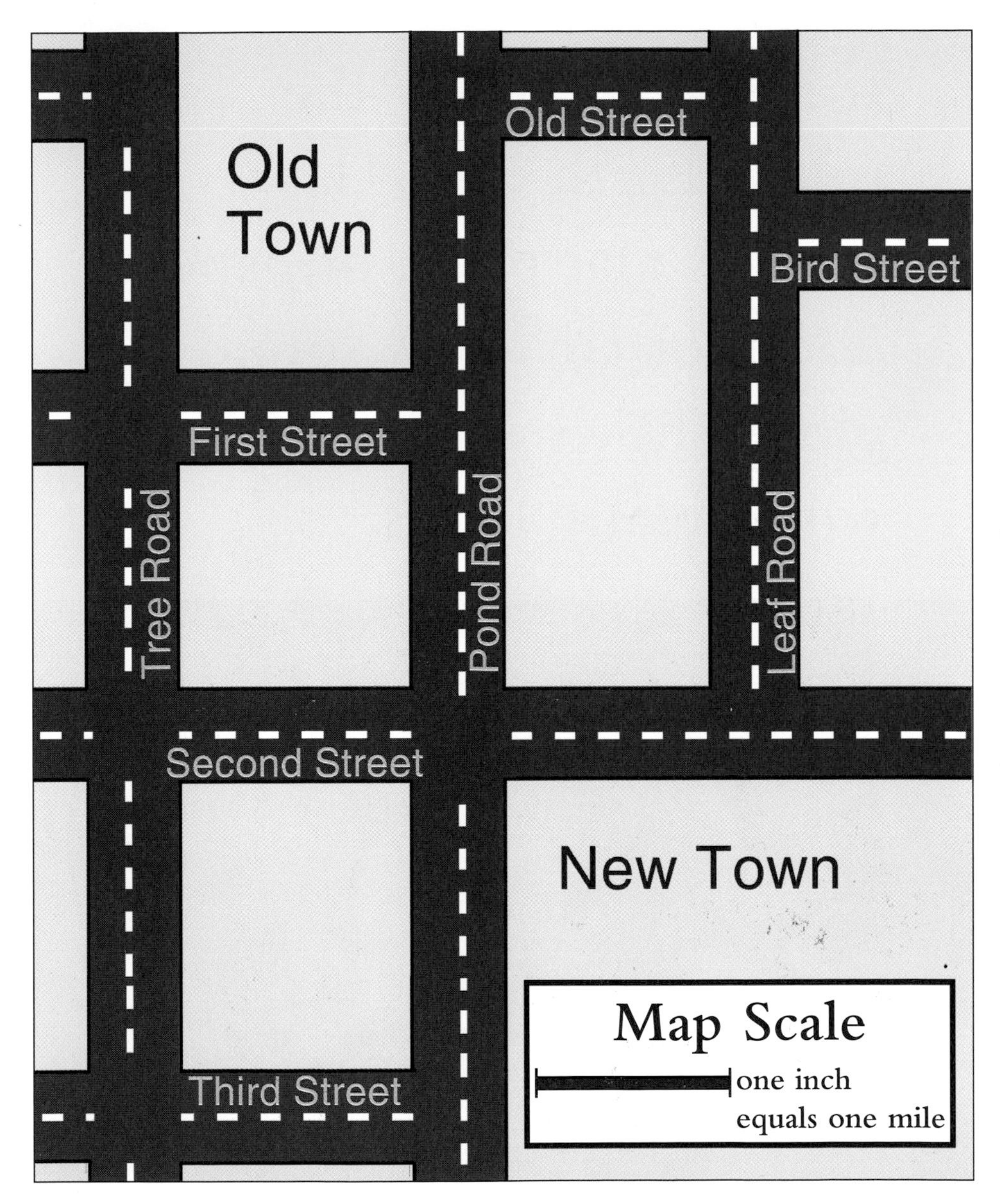
Old Town
Old Street
Bird Street
First Street
Tree Road
Pond Road
Leaf Road
Second Street
New Town
Third Street
Map Scale
one inch
equals one mile

It is hard to show the round Earth on a flat map. A flat piece of paper does not curve. A round globe shows us how the world really looks.

It curves like the Earth.

The top of the globe
shows us the part of Earth
called the North Pole.

The bottom of the globe shows us the South Pole.

The imaginary line that wraps around the middle of the globe is called the equator (ee-KWAY-tur).

Find the United States on a globe. Is it above or below the equator?

equator

It is fun to find places
on a globe. You can
travel around the world
with just your finger!

Words You Know

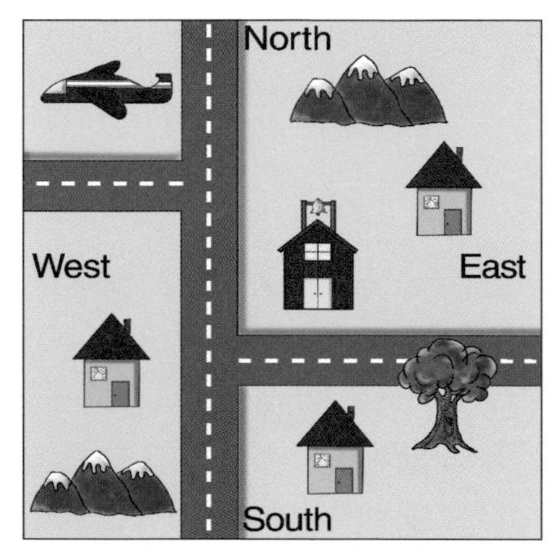

directions

equator

globe

map

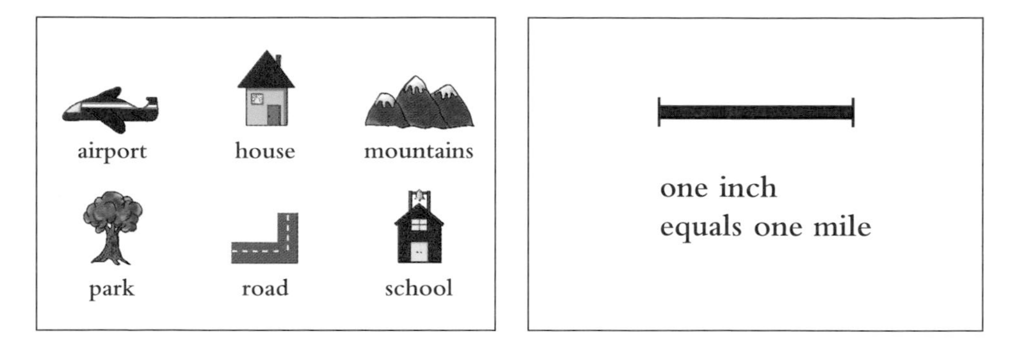

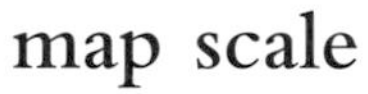

map legend

map scale

North Pole

South Pole

symbols

Index

About the Author

Carmen Bredeson is the author of twenty-five books for children. She lives in Texas and enjoys doing research and traveling.

Photo Credits

Photographs ©: Karen Nadalin Photography: 27, 30 top right; Nance S. Trueworthy: 4, 24, 25, 31 center right, center left; PhotoEdit: 3, 30 bottom right (Mary Kate Denny), 28 (Myrleen Ferguson), 7 (Robert Ginn), 6 (Michael Newman), cover (Jonathan Nourok); Stock Boston: 5 (Bob Daemmrich), 18 (John Elk III), 23 (NASA); Stone: 15 (Peter Correz), 22, 30 bottom left (Bob Krist).

Illustrations by A. Natacha Pimentel C.
Map by Bob Italiano.

FREE PUBLIC LIBRARY UNION, NEW JERSEY
3 9549 00306 3972